Heart and Soul
The Personal Reflections
of
Nielen McGarity

PDMI FREELANCE PUBLISHING PRESS

Heart and Soul
The Personal Reflections
of
Nielen McGarity

PDMI FREELANCE PUBLISHING PRESS
USA

PRINTED IN THE UNITED STATES OF AMERICA

Copyright Protected by My Original Works under IP Tech, a PDMI Company. Reference # 35109

First Edition, First Printing

ISBN-10: 061559476X

ISBN-13: 978-0615594767

All photography © 2012 by Nielen McGarity. All rights reserved and preserved.

Heart and Soul © made possible by and through PDMI Freelance Publishing Press LLC and EcoPreneur Press LLC.

Contact: pdmi@consultant.com www.pdmipublishing.com

PDMI Freelance Publishing Press
P.O. Box 56
Albertville, Alabama, USA 35950

PDMI logo is a registered trademark of (PDMI) Perceptional Design Management International (USA)

Published by PDMI (Perceptional Design Management International) USA By arrangement with the author.

All photographs © Copyright 2012 by Nielen McGarity. All rights reserved and preserved.

Dedication

My gratitude to the love of my life Lloyd McGarity Jr and to my children for their support of my love for poetry. To my brother Jake who always encourages me to follow my dreams. I also want to thank my friends Tony and Tracy Knight as well as PDMI publishing for their support and friendship.

In loving Memory
of my
Mother and Father
Marilyn and Charles Franklin

~ Reflective Contents ~

Our Love

As the sun shows
And the grass grows
As the moon shines
And the stars glow
Our love will always grow

Pure Love

Pure love is like a white rose
Glimmering in the morning sunlight

Pure love is like a mountain spring
Flowing with it's beauty so rare

Pure love is Gods love in his
unchanging loving way

Pure love is for now and always

Spring, Love and Things

My love for you is beautiful as the first day of spring

The flowers bloom and the birds begin to sing

My thoughts are filled with so many happy things

Oh how my love for you grows and grows and grows

Just as the sun shines and the moon glows

Personal Reflections

Summer Breeze

With the warm summers breeze
I feel your body so close to me

Oh how fast does my heart beat
Hand in hand we walk through the sand
I have not just a lover but also a friend

Oh how lucky I must be
To find that someone special just for me

I know that true love for you and
me will always and forever be

The Sun will Shine Today

The sun will shine today
So much more than yesterday

I feel the warmth of the sun on my face
Which gives me new hope to embrace

And that puts a smile on my face
That helps me get through another day

Personal Reflections

When your Eyes met Mine

When your eyes met mine
And we kissed for the first time

Oh how that makes my heart beat
With the sound of wind chimes

With your hand in mine
Together we will stand strong
So shall we shine

Our love will sparkle now and
Throughout the test of time

Where I need to Be

As the stars shine so bright
And the warmth of the sun shines on my face

I am working on where in life I really need to be

Sometimes the ocean rolls
Tossing me to and fro

And I feel like a lost ship way out to sea
And I wonder can this really be

Is there some greater purpose out there
Waiting for me
Or is it right in front of me
That I just cannot see

Personal Reflections

Which way to Go

Sometimes the wind will blow
and the snow will flow

It's had to know which way to go
The heart in one directions
And the head in another

It seems there is no place to go
When shall the sun show on where I need to go

Your Smile

Everytime I see your smile
I know that when the storms are blowing
I can feel another mile

Your smile warms my heart so
I would be warm even if it were 30 below

I know that on you I can depend
Thank you so much for being my friend

A Brighter Tomorrow

The sun will shine again
Even though there is rain

And the stars seen so far away
When really they are closer than they seem

The aches of your heart seems as though
They will last forever

But in time the pain will fade
And there will be a brighter tomorrow

Always Near

I went to be with the lord today
He needed my help and gave me angel wings

He lent me for a little while so that I could touch
Your lives and bring to you a smile

So dry the tears from your eyes
And always remember
In your heart I will always be near

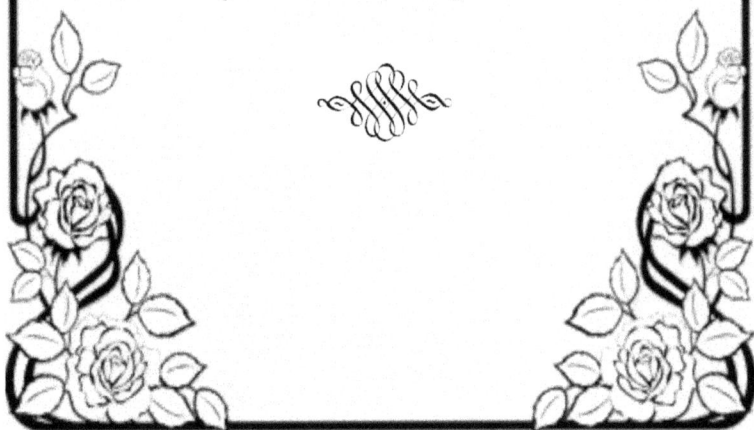

Personal Reflections

Dreams Come True

You mean the world to me
Without your love where would I be

Your on my mind both day and night
When I see you in my mind I feel alright

I long to see the twinkle in your eyes
And feel the touch of your embrace
That makes me feel safe

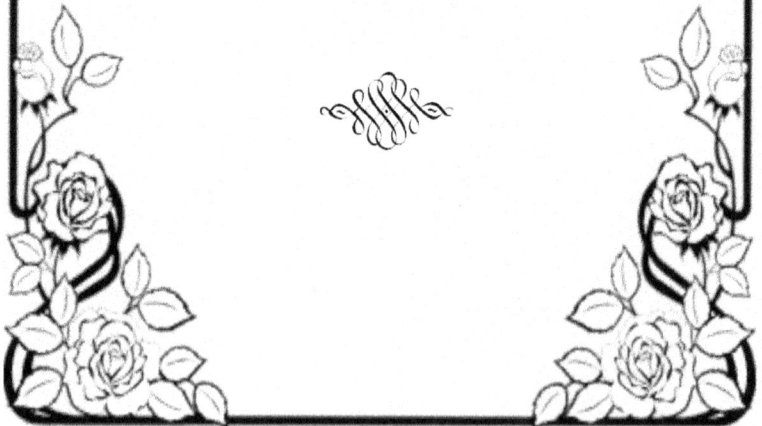

Even Though

Even though from time to time
It seems we are miles apart
You have always been my heart

We have had great times
Some sad times

But our love sees us through
I could not imagine my life without you

Forever my Heart
(In loving memory of Bobby Barrett)

Your eyes sparkle like shinning stars
It doesn't matter where you are

You will always be in my heart
Time may pass
But you being part of my heart will forever last

Friends like You

Friends like you are near and dear to my heart
When I see your smile it helps me get through

You've shared my sadness
You being there fills my heart with gladness

I am glad that I have friends like you
Because treasures like you are way to few

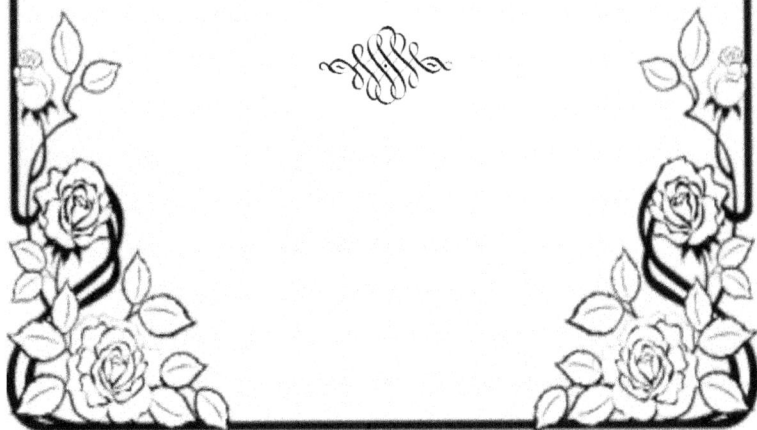

Personal Reflections

My Heart and Soul

You are my heart and soul
Without your love I would be so cold

You are on my mind both day and night
When I'm in your arms I know I'll be alright

I know that true love for you and me
Will always and forever be

Hospital Blues

Lying here in my hospital room and feeling so blue
All my thoughts are filled with you
Dreaming of the day when you are near

My heart is weak but your love makes me strong
Having your voice on the phone fills my heart with a song

Oh my darling I am so blessed
That you were sent to me from God who truly cares

Together we are strong and the world will see
Our love that will be
Now and for always

Personal Reflections

I Love you More

I love you more than the thousand stars in the sky
Taller than the highest mountain you can climb

More than the sands of the seas
Even more than all of these
Is how my love for you will always be

Jesus Christ is Coming Soon

Jesus Christ is coming Soon
So please give your heart to him

He stands at the door knocking
He wants to come in and cleanse you of your sins

All you have to do is ask him to come in
And forgive you of your sins

Personal Reflections

Jesus is my one true Friend

Jesus is my one true friend that I can really put my trust in
He holds my hand through rough times
He gives me joy and peace of mind

He's my strength when I'm not so strong
He keeps my heart always with a song

That's why I love Jesus so much
Because he's my one true and special friend

Little Blessings

The sun shines so brightly today
We can go outside and play

It's a joyest sound to hear my children swing and play
We have so much to be thankful for this I will say

My little children is such a blessing now and for always

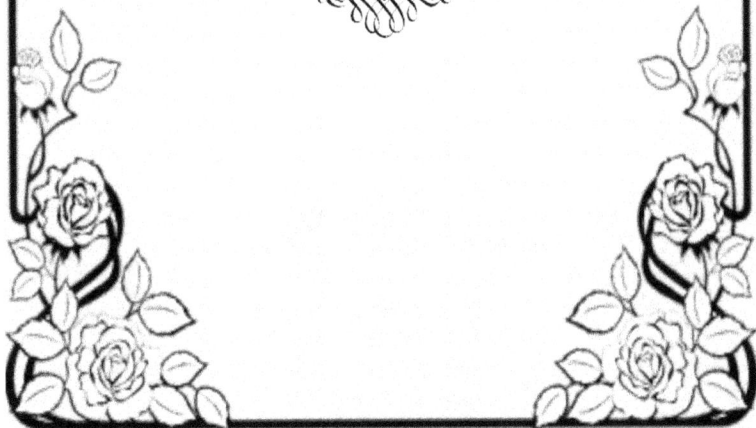

Personal Reflections

Missing you Dear

I love you so much dear
I think of you and wish you were near

Our hearts beat as one you see

You are always in my thoughts
And on my mind constantly

Every time I think of your smile so sweet
I feel like I could jump high up in the air at least 10 feet

My love for you will forever and always be

My Guardian Angels

My guardian angels are watching over me
They brought me back when my heart was weak

I know that god from up above
Knew how much I would be missed
And how much that I am loved

Thank you God from up above
For sending me back to the family that I love

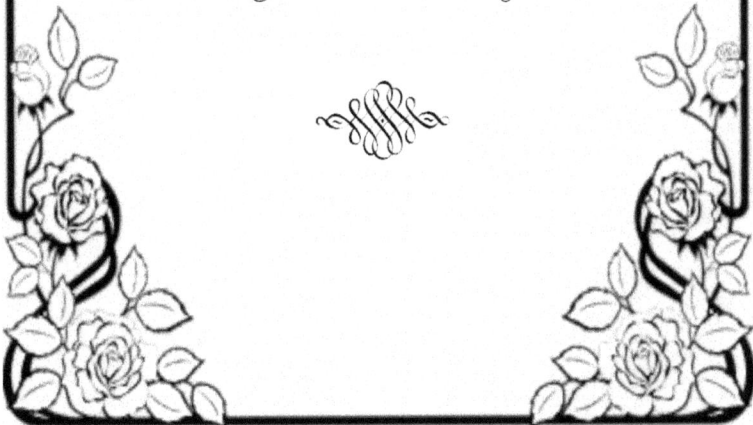

Personal Reflections

My Love for You

My love for you is stronger than the strength of the ocean
Longer and deeper than the depth of the sea

Purer than the honey of bees
Softer than the touch of the breeze

Even stronger than all of these
That's how much my love for you will always be

My Son, My Soldier

(Written for my son John Wesley Dickens)

My son is a soldier now
In service to God and to his country

He left me home a short while ago
He trained to be a soldier and took an oath

An oath to protect our freedom
Where ever in the U.S. We choose to go

We owe a great deal to our soldiers you see
With out them the freedom we have just would not be

Personal Reflections

Our Love Will Always Be

Our love is high as a mountain

Deeper than the ocean

Brighter than the stars

As soft as a spring breeze

That is how our love will always be

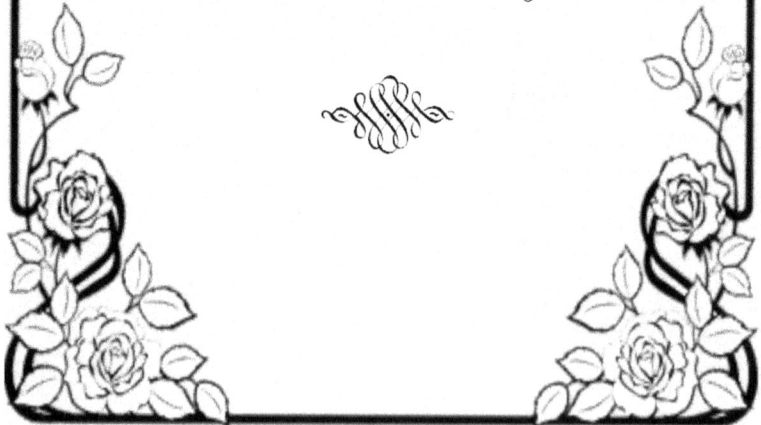

You, Me and a Cup of Coffee

You, me and a cup of coffee
What sweet words could there be

Sitting across the table
Your hand in mine

I am so in love with you
It makes me shine

Personal Reflections

Spring is in the Air

Spring is in the air
The flowers of fragrance everywhere

I lay on the grass that is so green
And I feel so serene

The sky is so blue with white puffy clouds
That I can see animals like a giraffe, a koala bear and
a kangaroo

Spring is my favorite time of year
It feels me with such cheer

Soft Summer Day

On a soft summer day
A warm breeze blowing through my hair

I think of your smile
Your hand in mine
And the twinkle in your eye

My love for you will stand the test of time

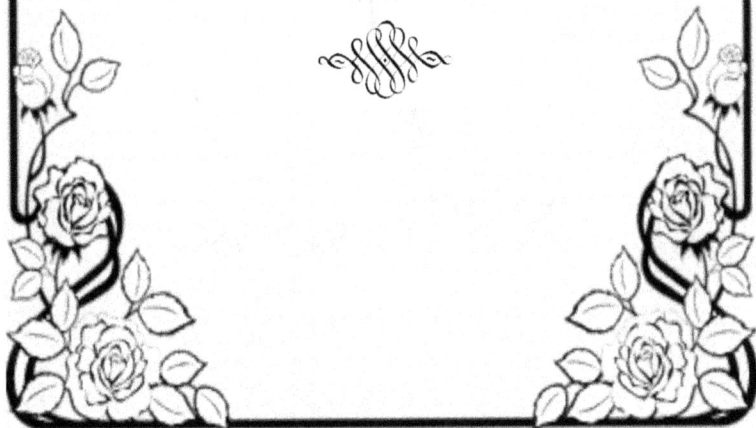

Personal Reflections

Personal Handwritten

Reflections

all girls are princesses

all girls are princesses that deserve a crown of their own

with pearls, satin gowns and shinny glass slippers to show

we cant forget a carrige to travel where ever the want to go

So each time I see my sweet girls I want them to know they are mommies little princesses

Soft Summers day

On a soft Summers day

a warm breeze blowing through my hair

I think of your smile, ~~and~~ your hand in mine
and the twinkle in your eye
my love for you will stand the test of time

A Brighter tomorrow

The sun will shine again
Even though there is rain

And the stars seen so far away
when really they are closer than they see

The ache's of your heart seems as though
they will last forever

But in time the pain will fade and
there will be a brighter tomorrow

Always Near   12/11/04

I went to be with the Lord today

He needed my help and gave me
angles wings

He lent me for a little while so
that I could touch your lives
and bring to you a smile

so dry the tear from your eyes
and always remember in your
heart I will always be near!

Dreams come True

you mean the world to me

without your love where would I be

your on my mind both day and night

when I see you in my mind I feel alright

I long to see the twinkle in your
eyes and feel the touch of your
embrace that makes me feel safe

Forever my heart

your eyes sparkle like shinning stars

It does'nt matter where you are

you will always be in my heart

Time may pass but you being part
of my heart will forever last

"In loving memory of Bobby Barrett"
"from one poet to another"

Even Though

Even though from time to time
It seems we are miles apart

you have always been my heart

we have had great times
and some sad times

But our love sees us through
I could not emagine my life
without you

Friends like you

Friends like you are near and dear
to my heart

when I see your smile it helps me
get though

you've shared my sadness
and yourbeing there fills my heart
with gladness

I am glad that I have friends like you

Because treasures like you are way to few

My Heart and Soul! Feb 7th 2010

You are my Heart and soul

without your love I would be so cold

you are on my mind both day and night

when I'm in your arms I know I'll
be alright

I know that true love for you
and me will always and forever be

Hospital Blues

Lying here in my hospital room
and feeling so blue

all my thoughts are filled with you
and dreaming of the day when
you are near

My heart is weak but your love
makes me strong and hearing your
voice on the phone fills my
heart with a song

oh my darling I am so blessed that
you were sent to me from God
who truly cares

Together we are strong and the
world will see our love that
will for now and for always be

I love you more

I love you more than the
thousand stars in the sky

taller than the highest mountain
you can climb

more than the sands of the seas

even more than all of these
is how my love for you will
always be

Jesus Christ is comaming
soon

so please give your heart to him

It stands at the door knocking
he wants to come in and cleans
you of your sins

all you have to do is ask him to
come in and forgive you of your sins

Jesus is my one true Friend 7/25/84

Jesus is my one true friend
that I can really put my trust in

He holds my hand through rough
times and gives me joy and
peace of mind

He's my strength when I'm not so
strong

He keeps my heart always with
a song

Thats why I love Jesus so much
is because he's my one true ~~friend~~
and special friend

Little Blessings   3/30/09

The sun shines so brightly today

we can go outside and play

Its a joyest sound to hear my
children swing and play

we have so much to be thankful
for this I will say

my little children is such a
blessing now and for always

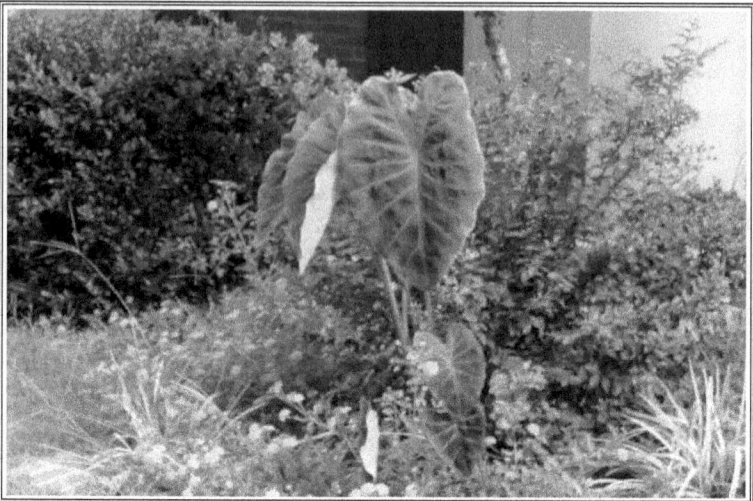

Spring, love, and Things 2/25/10

My love for you is beautiful
as the first day of spring

The flowers blooms and the birds
begin to sing

My thoughts are filled with so
many happy thing

Oh how my love for you grows
and grows and grows

Just as the sun shines and the
moon glows

Our Love

Our love is high as a mountain

Deeper than the ocean

Brighter than the stars

as soft as a spring breeze

That is how our love will
always be

My Guardian Angels   12/10/04

My Guardian angels are wathing over me

They brought me back when my heart was weak

I know that God from up above knew how much I would be missed and how much that I am loved

Thank you God from up above for sending me back to the family that I love!

Missing You Dear

I love you so much dear

I think of you and wish you
were near

Our hearts beat as one you see

You are always in my thoughts
And on my mind Constantly

Every time I think of your smile
so sweet

I feel like I could jump high
up in the air at least 10 feet

My love for you will forever
and always be!

My Son My Soldier 8/26/07

My son is a soldier now

In service to God and to his Country

He left from home a short while ago

He train to be a soldier and he
took an oath

an oath to protect our freedom
Were ever in the us We choose to go

We owe a great deal to our soldiers
you see

with out them the freedom shere just would
not be!

written for my son
John Wesley Dickerso

My love for you

My love for you is stronger than the strength of the ocean

longer and deeper than the depth of the sea

purer than the honey of bees

softer than the touch of the breeze

Even stronger than all of these
thats how my love for you will
always be!

Summer Breeze

With the warm summers breeze
I feel your body so close to me

Oh how fast does my heart beat

Hand in hand we walk through
the sand

I have not just a lover but also a
friend

Oh how lucky I must be

To find that someone special just
for me

I know that true love for you and
me will always and forever Be

Where I need to be

As the stars shine so bright
and the warmth of the sun shines on my face

I am working on where in life I really
need to be

Sometimes the ocean rolls tossing me
to and fro

and I feel like a lost ship way out to sea

And I wonder can this really be

Is there some greater purpose out there
waiting for me

Or is it right in front of me that I
just cannot see!!

Which way to go

Sometimes the wind will blow
and the snow will flow
It's hard to know which way to go
The heart in one direction
and the heart in another
and it seems there is no place to go
when shall the sun show or where
I need to go

pure love

pure love is like a white Rose
glimmering in the morning sunlight

pure love is like a mountain spring
flowing with it's beauty so rare

pure love is Gods love in his
unchanging loving way

pure love is for now and always

When your eyes meet mine

when your eyes meet mine

and we kiss for the first time

Oh how that makes my heart
beat with the sound of wind chimes

with your hand in mine together
we will stand strong and so shall
we shine

Our love will sparkle now and
throughout the test of time

Our Love

As the sun shows
And the grass grows

As the moon shines
And the stars glow

Our love will Always grow

The sun will shine today

The sun will shine today
so much brighter than yesterday

I feel the warmth of the sun
on my face which gives me new
hope to embrace

and that puts a smile on my face
that helps me get through another day

Your Smile

Every time I see your smile

I know that when the storms are
blowing I can face another mile

Your smile warms my heart so

I would be warm even if it were
30° below

I know that on you I can depend

Thank you so much for being my frien

www.ingramcontent.com/pod-product-compliance
Lightning Source LLC
Chambersburg PA
CBHW071024040426

42443CB00007B/924